MCR

MAY 0 4 2021

D1383444

BROTHERLY LOVE

Written by Dr. Michael Allen and
Gilbert D. Allen

Brotherly Love
Copyright © 2020
Published by Tgosketch Illustration
All rights reserved.
ISBN: 978-1-7344187-7-4
All rights reserved. No portion of this book may be reproduced in any form without permission from the publisher, except as permitted by U.S. copyright law.

This book is dedicated to:

There have been countless mentors and people that have supported us over the years. We are grateful for you as well as all of our family members and loved ones. Each of you, in your own way, aided in our process of fully embracing the values connected to the bright side of hope. We see you, completely accept you, and we love you. You have reminded us that no matter how much darkness may lie ahead, there is always light lurking waiting to be discovered. The richness embedded in Zion, Waukegan, and Valparaiso has forever etched itself in the foundation of who we have become. The gifts of time, education, and opportunities are things we are grateful to have shared with each of you. Whether near or far, wherever we go, we take the authenticity of these invaluable experiences with us, and we will never forget that we are because of who you are.

— Dr. Michael Allen and Gilbert D. Allen

PREFACE

D r. Michael Allen and Gilbert D. Allen come from extreme poverty. Their parents battled drug addiction. Their siblings were homeless and displaced at various points during their childhood. Gilbert is five years younger than Michael—and the youngest. Gilbert was living between multiple places when Michael went to college. Michael had just finished football practice and a team dinner when he received a call from his brother Gilbert in the fall. Gilbert said there was a *void* he was feeling. It was a hard conversation for Michael; his brother was sobbing. Michael's college football team was having a magical championship season winning but his baby brother was hurting.

Ultimately Michael consoled his brother, connected to his brother. Still, it got worse. Michael decided to go get his brother and take him with him to college. Gilbert finished high school while Michael was in college. Gilbert was reading at the fourth-grade level as a sophomore in high school. They had to navigate his readiness (in the northwestern part of Indiana at a majority white school). There was segregation within the community. Very few people thought Gilbert would finish high school—now he has his master's degree in social work and is working on a doctorate in counseling, community care, and trauma. Gilbert works as a social work supervisor; Michael has a doctorate in educational leadership and is an elementary school principal.

This book is about bonds—especially their bond as brothers, and the importance of mentors, related or not. This book is a glimpse into the collective political correctness eroding genuine connections. It also is much about love, fond dreams, and what it means to give back to marginalized people. Their goals are to encourage people to believe and hope.

They give insight, perspective, and share their journey within these pages. "It would be disrespectful to the journey if we don't give back," Michael said. "We have lessons to give back to humanity."

The voices of Gilbert *and* Michael make it clear society is ill-equipped. It's a beautiful struggle. Diversity is good. They hope you'll read this—and participate by reaching out to someone.

CONTENTS

CHAPTER 1

"When you arrive at school, learning the lessons will be hard because there is a game going on here, and you don't have the rules on your card."
— *Gilbert*

Gilbert glanced at the paper in front of him, and it was another "F." It's not that he wasn't trying; school was just harder for him than it was for the other kids. The bell rang, and something told him to get up and go home, but he decided he wanted to try one more time to get a passing grade.

"Mrs. Campbell," Gilbert said shyly. "I would like to discuss my grades with you if you have a minute."

His teacher rolled her eyes and looked up at him. She waited dramatically like she always did when she felt her time was being wasted.

"Gilbert, hear me out. We've been through this. Your grades have not been improving, and at the rate you are going, they won't anytime soon. No talks with me or tutoring lessons are going to fix that. Why don't you save us both the time and just go home?"

He saw it coming. He shouldn't be hurt, but he couldn't help but feel like it shouldn't be this difficult to get support with school work. It was the same old experience he had with every teacher, and he was tired of it, but he wasn't going to give up.

"I'm just trying to be better," he said softly. "It's hard for me. I can barely see the board, and most of the time, things don't make sense to me, and it takes a lot to get things to make sense and …"

"Let me stop you right there," Mrs. Campbell interrupted. "You're not doing well because you're just not that smart. There's nothing wrong with you. You're not going to be a brainiac. Just focus on sports, that's what you're good at."

It was comments like this that sometimes made

him feel defeated and unseen for who he was even though he was good at sports.

Sports was the one thing that he and his family were good at. Gilbert was a sophomore and was excited about starting on the varsity football team. He loved playing, but being on varsity meant longer practices, traveling farther for games, and being under more pressure to be great. Because of this, he needed even more support, and that support would come from his big brother. Fortunately for Gilbert, his older brother, Michael, was good at staying on top of things. Gilbert knew Michael was a great example to follow. He was the only one so far to go to college, and Gilbert missed Michael in times like these. He knew he needed his big brother, especially since he felt like no one supported him at school.

He hung his head and started for home. He wanted to be more than just a ballplayer or an athlete. He wanted to be something bigger than that. When he got home, he prepared to tell his sister Tasha about another "F."

"*She'll get me,*" he thought to himself. "Everyone says, just try your hardest. Give it all you got. So I do, and stuff like this happens!"

Gilbert decided to vent to Tasha when he got home. "Mhmm," she replied, equally overwhelmed with trying to support her brother and trying to get her newborn daughter to stop crying as she did every time he was upset about his grades.

Gilbert knew she was trying; she had made the sacrifice herself to take care of him, feed him, and provide clothes for him, but she didn't know how to be there for him the way his older brother did. That didn't matter, though, because all he had now was his sister. His brother Michael had gone away to college.

As the youngest of five, Gilbert had heard all the stories about things he wished he hadn't. He knew his parents battled drug addiction and struggled to provide what he and his siblings needed.

Some of his earliest days were spent with his siblings trying to find food. He remembered the fear of seeing roaches and mice in his family's bathroom and the countless nights without water. He could recall the feeling of shame when their family's electricity was shut off. He saw his older siblings step up countless times, even when they didn't have a place to stay. He knew he should be grateful for that. He also knew that by being in college, his big brother was making something of himself. Where they came from, college was rarely something people got to experience. Unfortunately, with the grades he received, Gilbert felt there was no way to experience this kind of opportunity.

CHAPTER 2

*"You will appear all alone, empty, and about to fall.
That's when you will walk into the apartment and
answer a magical call."*

— *Gilbert*

Gilbert often wished he had someplace quiet to escape to, but the screams of his new niece were bigger than the one-bedroom apartment he shared with his sister, Tasha, and her boyfriend.

"I'm gonna go take a walk," he said as he grabbed his coat and walked out the door.

Gilbert loved to take walks outside. The cool air was refreshing, and it helped him think. He liked watching the people on the streets. He just knew their lives were better than his. On his way back home, he saw one of the older boys from the projects, Cory.

Cory's mom passed away from cancer when he was in high school, and he didn't have any relatives or family friends to take him in. While he was athletic and strong in science, he didn't get good grades in his other classes. After his mother's passing, he believed his only two options were selling drugs or going through the foster care system as a teenager. He decided to drop out of high school and sell drugs.

Gilbert had been warned several times by his family to stay away from him, but that was hard because Cory was a natural leader and a known drug dealer in the neighborhood. He was always around looking for more corner boys. Of course, he was one of Cory's main prospects, and he had wanted Gilbert to join him for a while now. Gilbert was aware of this, but he knew that his brother Michael would be so disappointed in him, but he also knew that the money he would make would provide a better life for his sister, niece, and himself.

He decided to take the long way to avoid Cory and his crew. The wind blowing through the big trees took his mind off of Cory for the time being. When he got home, his niece was asleep. Finally, he could have some time to ask his sister for help with his problems at school.

"Hey, sis?" Gilbert said. Tasha, who had just found a few seconds of peace and quiet, was lying on the couch. Before she could muster up the energy to respond, he followed by saying, "Can I ask you something about my work if I need your help?"

"Sorry, baby bro," she replied with her eyelids closed. "I'm too tired. Why don't you call Michael?"

He picked up the phone and called his brother. Gilbert told Michael all about school and his grades. He talked about how he felt his teachers had no interest in helping him, and all about Cory and his crew. He also discussed how he was starting to question his ability to play sports and do well in his classes. Just as he finished saying, "Nobody ... I mean nobody understands me ..." he heard nothing on the other end on the phone for a few seconds.

"Michael," Gilbert asked, "Are you still there?"

"Yeah, I'm still here," Michael said. "I love you, little bro. I want you to stay strong. One day things won't be like this anymore. If things don't get better, I will bring you here with me. I know I'm far away now, but you can always call me if you need to. As far as your homework goes, why don't you tell me what you are working on, and I'll see if I can help you out."

Gilbert started telling Michael about his homework, and they stayed on the phone until everything was done. When they said their goodbyes, Gilbert repeated his brother's words in his head, *"One day things won't be like this anymore…"* He didn't know how, but he trusted his brother. *"Everything will be okay,"* he said to himself as he drifted to sleep.

CHAPTER 3

"You will walk into the office and get the news that changes everything. Your coach will utter the word 'ineligibility' — making you scream."
— Gilbert

The next day school was a lot like the first, and so was the next day, and the day after that. Gilbert was starting to get down. His grades weren't getting any better, and the lockers in the hallway seemed to be closing in on him. Even when he sat in class, he felt invisible—though his friends were still laughing at his jokes, and he tried his best to pass his tests. He would often replay the words of his brother, Michael. But those encouraging words his brother said weeks ago began to feel a little different, and his hopes for a better tomorrow started to fade.

The once-encouraging words he was left with from his brother started to have a different impact on Gilbert. After school on Gilbert's way home, he became very angry with Michael and his words from their last conversation. *"Easy for him to say things will be better. He knew what life was like here and left me anyway,"* Gilbert thought as he walked up the stairs, awaiting the screams of his niece.

He talked to his sister about how he felt. She nodded apologetically. Tasha hated seeing her baby brother so upset.

"At least you still got football, you know? I realize things are hard. Life gets rough, but just hold on to the things that matter, the things you love," she said.

The next day at football practice, Gilbert noticed some guys fighting in the middle of the street. He knew he should stay out of it until he spotted one of his other brothers, Brandon.

His coach yelled at him to not leave practice, but Gilbert couldn't help himself. "That's my brother, coach," he yelled as he ran toward his brother anyway.

Gilbert didn't see much of Brandon. He knew that he belonged to the streets now. Growing up, he learned that family comes first, even when you have to choose between helping family versus helping yourself—it's tough. After things had calmed down, and he knew his brother was safe, Gilbert went back to practice. He didn't realize how much time had passed. He walked onto an empty field with his coach sitting in the bleachers, waiting for him.

"I told you to stay put." His coach said, reprimanding him as he gazed into the distance.

"I don't care who was out there, when you're on my field, on my time, you listen to me."

"But coach, I was just trying to help," said Gilbert.

"No," his coach interjected. "Save your excuses, you're suspended from this week's game." Gilbert couldn't believe his ears. As he watched his coach walk away, he knew he made a mistake, but he couldn't fight the tears of frustration as he headed to the locker room to gather his things.

Gilbert was too depressed to take advantage of his free time now that he was suspended. As a result, his grades suffered. Eventually, he was put on academic probation and wouldn't be able to play for the rest of the season.

Crushed and confused as to what to do next, he continued to spiral. His sister noticed her brother was off and called Michael. Within weeks, Michael was back. The whole time Michael was gone, he was working on a bigger plan to help Gilbert. When he got home, he told Gilbert he had gained custody of him, and that they would be living together in Indiana where Michael was in college.

Gilbert was enrolled in a new school close to Michael's college. Things seemed to be looking up for Gilbert.

The night they arrived at Michael's apartment, Gilbert had his own bed. For the first time, he believed things were going to be different just like Michael said.

Later that night, he overheard his brother on the phone.

"I hope I'm not in over my head. I want to be there for Gilbert, but I'm in school myself. I just hope this wasn't a mistake."

Gilbert knew Michael risked a lot to take him in. He promised himself he wouldn't let his big brother down.

CHAPTER 4

"You feel tremendous fear, pressure, and doubt on the drive. You will wonder whether you have the right tools long after you arrive."
— *Michael*

Gilbert enrolled in a new school. He quickly realized the issues he had at home were replaced by a brand new set of problems in this alternate world. He walked the halls and couldn't help but notice a sea of people that looked nothing like him. Gilbert tried not to let it bother him; after all, his brother made a huge sacrifice taking him in.

Although things were different, he was welcomed with open arms. He was even invited to try out for the school's track team!

Gilbert decided to try out for the track team after school. He didn't even realize he hadn't asked Michael for permission. Instead of getting home at 4 p.m., like Michael was expecting. Gilbert got home around 6:30 p.m., and was met by an anxious brother.

"Where were you?" Michael shouted as he walked in the door.

"I tried out for the track team. I didn't think you'd mind," Gilbert said. He didn't understand Michael's visible frustration. He remembered the area they were staying in now was much nicer than where they both grew up, and in a way, he was right. There were no gangs on the streets or people selling drugs in alleys.

"I'm glad you're making friends and trying out for sports, but there's something I need you to understand," Michael said. "The area we live in now doesn't have as many people like us as home does. Sure, the schools are nicer, and the help you'll get from your teachers is much better. But that doesn't change the fact that we look different, and sometimes people will treat us differently because of the color of our skin."

He hoped he was making sense but also didn't want to discourage his baby brother.

"It's just us out here, so we must always be on the same page. I need to know where you are at all times, so I can make sure you're safe. Now about track, remember that there's more to you than being good at sports. I told you before, one day things will start to look up, and now look at you. Just trust me and stay strong. There's greatness inside you, don't let anything distract you from that."

Gilbert realized how fortunate he was to have a big brother who would fight for him the way Michael did. He knew he would have to adjust to his new world, but he also knew with his brother by his side, he could do anything.

CHAPTER 5

"At first, things will quickly get a lot better. Then, the season will change, and you will experience different weather."
— Gilbert

Gilbert was taking to his new school and was excelling on the track. He broke numerous school records and was gaining tons of confidence. However, the ghosts of Gilbert's academic past were not too far behind. One day, Michael received a call to bring his brother to a meeting with one of Gilbert's teachers.

In the meeting, the brothers were informed that Gilbert was being placed on academic probation and would not compete in the next big track meet. Also, the board was concerned with why Gilbert was living with Michael instead of at home with his parents.

At home, Gilbert broke down. "As soon as things start looking up, something comes along to tear me down. I'm tired of fighting," he said.

Michael hugged his brother and told him, "Nothing I can do or say will take away what just happened. It's okay to feel whatever you are feeling, especially since we both know how hard you worked for this. As hard as it may be to hear, this is one of those situations where your response is much more important than what happened to you."

Michael was motivating both Gilbert and himself at this point. "Just focus on getting your grades up, I'll handle the board..."

Michael helped Gilbert study. He used games and activities to assist his brother in understanding his school work. They created goals and charts to track the important things for each day, week, and month. Michael's only requirement was that his brother gave it his all. Each time that Gilbert accomplished a goal, he developed more self-confidence.

In no time, Gilbert's grades started improving. His classes seemed easier, his homework didn't take as long, and school itself became much more enjoyable.

Meanwhile, Michael was fighting the board about his custody agreement and trying to explain why it was best that Gilbert stayed with him. He made many phone calls to whoever would listen and attended many meetings with teachers, coaches, and the board, pushing to make sure that his brother was treated fairly. Finally, there was an agreement, and

Gilbert was eligible to play football at the beginning of the season! Michael was relieved things worked in his brother's favor. He knew that the move and playing football were important to keep him focused on school.

CHAPTER 6

"Some will cheer, and others will shout.
Some will believe, and others will doubt.
Some will show love, and others will show hate.
Some will be patient, and others cannot wait."
— Michael

With his grades looking good and a new football season waiting for him, Gilbert was ready to take on junior year of high school. He felt the worst of his troubles were behind him.

Gilbert put the football team on his back. He became a star overnight. Newspapers were printed with his picture on the front page, and people came from all over the state to interview him about his success.

He felt like a celebrity. When his team won, Gilbert was treated like a king. People would let him and his teammates eat in almost any restaurant in town for free.

But, when they lost, Gilbert got the worst of it. People would drive by the apartment he shared with Michael and throw eggs and other food on the windows and doors when they were not home. Gilbert even encountered a horrific experience at an away game. Each time he ran with the ball, the opposing crowd would scream and call him the N-word repeatedly. The opposing team would then poke their fingers in his eyes, and kick and punch him.

Michael was outraged! He immediately went to tell the security in charge of the game but was even more inflamed after they refused to do anything about it.

It was a hard lesson for both of them. Gilbert had never experienced anything like this, having grown up in a community where most of the people looked like him and shared many of his experiences.

Gilbert cried to his brother that night, "I just don't

understand how people can be so cruel. I don't deserve this! Nobody even tried to stop it! They all saw. I know they all saw!"

Gilbert had faced challenges but he wasn't prepared for something like this and neither was his brother. He didn't feel like a part of a team as neither the coach nor his teammates helped or protested. As he lay still feeling the pain of his wounds, he wondered if it was worth playing for at all.

"I know," Michael said softly, overwhelmed with sadness for his brother. "I can't imagine how you feel, and I can't promise I can make it better, but I know quitting isn't the right choice. We'll get through this together."

The next morning, they exercised and journaled about the experience after breakfast. While that didn't change the pain or make it go away, they learned how to move forward. Michael often played uplifting music for Gilbert, and they read books together to help them deal with the level of racism that they both were experiencing.

CHAPTER 7

"Finally, the end of college is here and your dreams of helping people once again appear." — *Michael*

While Gilbert was dealing with the pressure of getting through high school in a new environment with all new challenges, Michael's college career was coming to an end. Just as Gilbert had to make critical decisions about his future, so did his big brother. Michael knew it was time to find what he was passionate about and figure out the course for the rest of his life. As he watched his brother go off to school, he began to realize his true passion. He believed that his purpose was to be a principal and help kids just like his brother. He wanted to be a resource for kids who were struggling in school and at home. He understood that the best way he could give back to society was by working with kids who were unsure about their futures and those who didn't have a hope for tomorrow.

He decided to run his ideas by the principal at the school he worked for part-time.

"... and that's what I would love to do. So, what do you think?" Michael said, proudly concluding his ideas.

"I'm sorry," the principal muttered in between laughs. "I don't mean to be rude, but there is no way you could be a principal. Some dreams are meant to be just that. Now, if you're finished, I have actual work to get done."

Michael pulled into his apartment in disbelief. No one had ever told him what he couldn't do before. He did not like the feeling, so he sat in the car and took some deep breaths to try to control his breathing.

He thought to himself, *"I gotta stay in this moment and learn the lesson ... in through the nose. Out through the mouth. In through the nose. Out through the mouth."*

That night after his brother came home from

practice, Michael explained what happened to him that day in the principal's office. He told Gilbert how much it bothered him, and how much he appreciated his baby brother for being the one person who always believed in him.

Even though Michael didn't say that he was sad, Gilbert could feel how this situation affected his older brother. He knew that he was hurt by what happened, but he was unsure about how to respond. Michael was his hero, and he was the one person that he had known his entire life that could do anything he put his mind to.

Little did the principal know: her words ultimately motivated Michael and Gilbert.

After that, they both realized how much they needed each other. They were each other's support system and biggest fan. That night their bond grew even stronger.

Before Gilbert went to bed, Michael reminded him, "If you are bold enough to have a dream, believe in it, protect it, and never stop working toward it."

Michael was rejected because of how he looked. His principal didn't care that he had all As in his classes, worked hard to secure his brother's future, and took the steps needed to raise him. She saw a man whose skin was different from hers, whose hair was more unique than she could tolerate, and a threat to her belief system. Fortunately for Michael, he didn't care how she felt about him either.

CHAPTER 8

"You become a change agent when you can look inside you
and evaluate the things you do." — Michael

Gilbert had coaches from schools all over the country coming to his high school. He visited big schools like Indiana University, Purdue University, University of Illinois, Western Michigan University, and Northern Illinois University. He was overwhelmed with happiness thinking about his future and all the possibilities.

Despite the success, Gilbert struggled with overcoming his fears mostly in his mind. He questioned if he had the talent that was needed and the strength to overcome the obstacles. He thought about whether it was worth the risk. To support and motivate his brother and himself, Michael constantly posted positive quotes all around their apartment from famous people like India Arie, Lauryn Hill, Dr. Martin Luther King Jr., and Nelson Mandela.

To stay focused in competition, Michael and Gilbert developed a ritual. They made a pact to not compete in any game or sports activity without wearing something that reminded them of each other. Often, it was a t-shirt, socks, a wristband, or their lucky numbers.

Life for these brothers was never easy but they became comfortable exceeding people's expectations. Doing so was always the prize.

Gilbert went on to break records for his high school's football and track teams. In addition to his outstanding athletic accomplishments, his grades were steadily improving as well. His Fs were turning into As and Bs, and his love for learning grew along with his passion for sports. He still dealt with racism at school and in the community, but he persevered through it all and it paid off.

During his senior year, Gilbert was invited to the all-state team, where he met tons of college coaches and secured a spot at the University of St. Francis in

Fort Wayne, Indiana. He received a full-ride scholarship. He went on to play football in college and was cheered on every game by his brother, Michael.

He turned down the noise of the people trying to discourage him from being who he knew he was meant to be: someone special. He created a schedule to help study for his classes and was very successful. He played in championship football games all over the country during his college career.

Gilbert kept his promise to his brother but, more importantly, to himself. He graduated with honors and went on to earn his favorite award, the "Top Social Work Student" during his last year of college. He came to college as a standout football player, but he left as a man committed to making the world better by living out his purpose as a social worker.

CHAPTER 9

"You don't have to play the hand that you were dealt when you have the ability to change the cards, and you can use your scars to put you among the stars." — Michael

Michael started off his career as a teacher and coach in Chicago and eventually went on to make his dream become a reality when he became one of the youngest principals in the country. Michael wanted to be the best principal he could be so he continued his studies earning a master's and a doctorate degree.

As a principal, he was known for creating schools focused on relationships and doing what's best for his students while pushing them to follow their dreams. He treated them like his own children and made sure that each of them knew they mattered and were loved. Just like with Gilbert, it was important to Michael that his students knew that failure wasn't an option, and he was willing to do anything to ensure they succeeded. When Michael's students made mistakes, he rarely sent them home. Instead, he often kept them at school longer, teaching them how to make better choices by repairing the harm that their actions caused themselves and others.

He worked with his school team to create programs that helped many of his struggling middle school students advance to their correct grade, find jobs, and graduate on time.

He often had his brother, Gilbert, come to his schools to give his students motivational speeches, showing them firsthand how far they can go if they never give up. Michael stayed in communication with his brother, never forgetting the person he fought for, and who also fought for him.

CHAPTER 10

"Wherever you choose to go, whether grassy land or rugged terrain, be it Colorado's mountains or underneath the Amazon's rain, remember to always listen for the wind that says your name and trust that your dream will eventually carry you to your hall of fame."
— Michael and Gilbert

Michael and Gilbert realized that even though they started in a hard place, their journey through education helped them learn the power of knowledge and the importance of perseverance. They dedicated their time to figuring out how they could give back to the world they left: a world full of depression, violence, and drugs. A world that lacked opportunities because it was filled with distractions that prevented people from accomplishing something more. They believed that what was needed in the world was more love.

They traveled around the world, teaching many students like them valuable lessons, like the way that you treat others is a reflection of how you feel about yourself. They focused on four important things: finding positive mentors, being vulnerable enough to accept and let go of the unhealthy feelings inside, talking to counselors, and practicing mindfulness.

Mentors were a big part of Michael and Gilbert's success. People they looked up to helped them make sense of so many things and knew how to put them in contact with the right people to reach their goals.

In finding mentors, they also wanted to make sure that they carried out their mission to encourage children and adults to share the deepest parts of themselves with other people and let go of the unhealthy feelings that come with living through painful experiences.

They also helped others understand the power of talking to school counselors, social workers, and therapists to deal with the tough things people often go through each day.

Michael and Gilbert constantly reminded students that their difficult experiences are not proof something is wrong with them. Instead, they believe that going through tough times and situations actually could be a recipe for success.

These brothers worked together to help bring awareness to the importance of believing in yourself and the lengths you can go to when you decide no dream is worth sleeping on.

The End.

GLOSSARY

Academic probation. When a student's grades are below the required standard in order to participate in sports or extracurricular activities at a school, college or university.

Corner boy. A teen or young adult male growing up in an underprivileged area whose circumstances compel him to sell drugs on the corners.

Custody. To legally be responsible for the safety and care of another person.

Full-ride scholarship. An award for sports, activities or academics that covers the entire cost of attendance at a school, college or university.

Ineligibility. Disqualified or not allowed to participate in an event, sport or activity.

N-word. A nonoffensive way of using the word "nigger" which is one of the most racist terms used in the English language to belittle black people.

Pact. A promise or commitment, usually between two people that is mutually beneficial and fairly agreed upon.

Prospects. A person or group of people regarded as likely to succeed at something.

Protest. A statement or action expressing disapproval of or objection to something.

Purpose. The reason for which something is done or created or for which something exists.

Made in the USA
Coppell, TX
15 April 2021

53811395R00033